I0689325

DEATH IS A LOVELY DAME

Great Lines from the Golden Era of Crime Fiction

Edited by
Jeff Vorzimmer

Published by

Automat.Press
//automat.press
Austin, Texas USA

Design and layout by
¡caliente!design
//caliente.design
Austin, Texas USA

Death is a Lovely Dame
Edited by Jeff Vorzimmer
Automat.Press edition published June 2016

Automat Catalog #A007

ISBN: 978-0-9970150-3-4

V5.0

0 9 8 7 6 5 4 3 2 1b

Scoring for alternate qualification
SUB. TOTAL
X, 10, 9, 8 rings = 5
7 ring = 4
All other hits on silhouette = 3
TOTAL
MUNICIPAL POLICE
TRAINING COUNCIL
COMBAT TARGET
SCORE SHADED AREA K5 ONLY
To score duel target combat
course add the total of K5's
on both targets.
K5
K5
K5
K5
K5

Table of Contents

Introduction 9
A Note on the Quotes and Covers 15
Pumping Lead.......... 19
Ugly Words Like Blackmail and Murder.......... 25
Femmes Fatales.......... 31
Existential Angst.......... 39
Drinking, Smoking & Other Vices 51
I Like Women Warm to the Touch.......... 57
A Ticket to the Gas Chamber.......... 61
Down These Mean Streets 65
Never Trust a Man Who Doesn't Drink 71
Tough Guys with Ugly Mugs.......... 75
Dirty Money 81
Just Pull the Trigger.......... 87
Better Off Dead 91
Her Eyes Had Pain in Them 95
Out of the Sewer.......... 99
Black Coffee Hot as Hell..........103
She's Old Enough to Be Your Wife 107
A Sound of Distant Drums 111
Acknowledgments..........119
About the Editor..........123

Introduction

Don't expect an apology for the hardboiled crime fiction of my generation, though by today's standards, it was often nihilistic, savagely brutal, propagated racial stereotypes and was sexist, almost misogynistic. It merely has to be put in the context of mid-twentieth century, Cold War America. Readers who grew up with the existential angst of the atomic age understand this inherently, but consider that today half the population of this country was born after 1960.

To have grown up in mid-century America meant growing up in a predominantly white, male-dominated society where mutually-assured destruction by atomic weapons was not only likely, but seemingly imminent. There were no shortage of evil dictators around the world, but evil was close to home as well. It seemed that Americans had become inured to the increasing violence on our streets as exemplified by high-profile murder cases such as that of Kitty Genovese in 1964.

It was a different world than it is today. We went to the school of hard knocks. Corporal punishment was meted out for the least infraction, every schoolyard had a bully, there were air-raid drills and numerous childhood diseases. There was no such thing as a "time-out," "rethink," or "safe-place." You could get a poke in the nose just for a wisecrack.

After-school time was unsupervised and usually spent on the streets or in pool halls learning how to smoke and to look cool with a cigarette dangling from your mouth. We knew there were bad people in the world. That's why we didn't fall victim to predators as often as kids seem to these days, though there were just as many then, as now, maybe more. We were tough kids.

There were no doting school librarians or Scholastic Book Clubs to gently guide the reading habits of young minds. Our libraries were the drugstores and newsstands, with their racks of lurid paperbacks, pulp magazines and comic books. When you couldn't afford to feed your pulp habit, you acquired it by five-finger discount. It was as addictive as crack. Of course, you just had to stay one step ahead of the local constabulary and out of juvenile detention.

These paperbacks and magazines not only shaped our world view, but they appealed to us because they mirrored the world in which we lived and the bad people, the wise guys, we saw every day. Though we might have managed to stay out of jail ourselves, maybe even got a college education and eventually amounted to something, we never completely lost the pulp habit.

These books, of course, reflected the world in the aftermath of two world wars in which young men had to assimilate back into society after having experienced the horrors and inhumanity of war. The good guys in these stories were the private detectives such as Philip Marlowe, Mike Hammer and Shell Scott, who brought the good fight back home with them to the mean streets of New York and L.A.

The criminals were the guys who had nothing to come home to after the war but a sense that the world owed them something and was doomed anyway, so you might as well take what you could get, at any cost. The only things that mattered were the money, booze and dames that eased the pain of a seemingly imminent, inevitable death. They lived a little faster and died a little faster. In the end death comes anyway, whether it comes in a bed or in the electric chair or in the gas chamber.

Existential angst has been defined by the analogy of a man standing on the edge of a cliff who fears not so much the danger of falling off as much as the compulsion to throw himself off. That is the sense of doom that prevails throughout these novels.

There are, of course, other important elements that characterize the hardboiled crime novels of the period. What follows is a list of fourteen typical plot elements of the genre. Not all of them are necessary, except, of course, the first.

1. A crime (can precede the timeline of the narrative);
2. An unsympathetic protagonist (with whom you none-the-less identify);
3. A femme fatale;
4. Tough, wise-cracking dialogue;
5. Sexual tension;
6. A tough brutal thug (the nemesis) with an unusual torture technique;
7. An ironic plot twist or two;
8. A double-cross;
9. A sense throughout that all the characters are doomed;
10. Corrupt police officers or city officials;
11. Lots of rye whisky, black coffee and cigarettes;
12. A protagonist who is beaten up, shot, stabbed or least knocked unconscious;
13. A lurid cover featuring a scantily-clad woman in a compromising position; and,
14. A title with words such as "DEATH," "DEADLY," "MURDER," "GIRL," "WOMAN," "DAME," "GUN" or "NIGHT."

It should be noted that titles with words denoting the feminine gender such as "woman," "women," "dame," "girl(s)," "virgin," or "wife" appear more than twice as often as those denoting the male, such as "man," "men," "husband," or "boys." This, of course, was due simply to the fact that these books were targeted at young male readers.

The characters in these books—modern day paladins—served as role models for young men as the knights of Sir Walter Scott novels or the swashbuckling heroes of Alexandre Dumas had for previous generations. More often than not, these knights were rescuing damsels in distress.

Needless to say, a diet of pulp fiction doesn't breed metrosexual men who drink fruit-garnished cocktails with little umbrellas, mocha lattes from Starbucks, vape and eat nouvelle cuisine. No, guys like us prefer our whisky straight, coffee black, cigarettes unfiltered and our food from a diner.

We believe that the world is a constant struggle between good and evil, not between the evolved and the archaic, nor that the world could live in harmony if we could all sit around a campfire and sing Kumbaya.

The younger generation may perceive us as backward or barbaric, but we cannot and will not abandon our beliefs. They'll just have to wait for death to come for us and leave them to a world of their own creation. For better or worse.

Jeff Vorzimmer
Austin, Texas

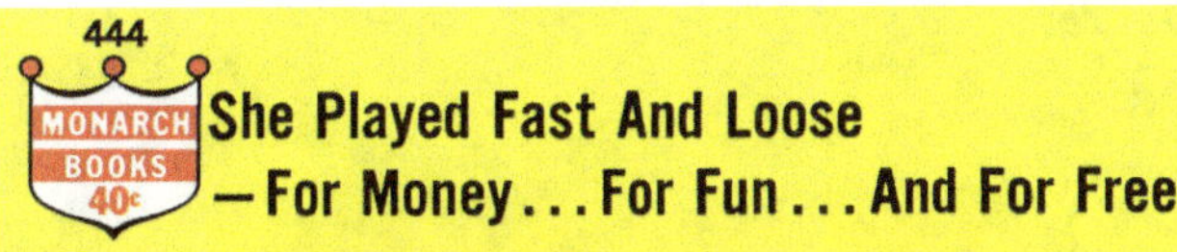
444
MONARCH
BOOKS
40¢
She Played Fast And Loose
—For Money...For Fun...And For Free

PLAY
IT HARD

Gil Brewer
First Publication Anywhere

s1085
35c
GOLD MEDAL BOOK
The living was high and the pickings came easy — till my one wild love became my sweet, slow death
MONA
LAWRENCE BLOCK

A Note on the Quotes and Covers

It's no coincidence that the majority of the covers and many of the quotes included here come from the books of one publisher, Fawcett Publications. Their Gold Medal line of paperback originals attracted some of the best young writers by offering higher royalties than traditional publishers. They also used talented artists such as Robert McGinnis and Barye Phillips to illustrate their covers.

Fawcett offered larger advances and paid royalties to authors based on the number of copies of books printed rather than on books sold. Since the Gold Medal line were original titles, that is, books being published for the first time as paperbacks and not as reprints of hardback titles, there were no royalties to be paid to the hardback publisher and Fawcett passed that portion of the royalties on to the authors.

Many of the greatest contemporary writers got their start making real money with Gold Medal paperbacks including Lawrence Block, Donald Westlake, Elmore Leonard, Ed McBain, William Goldman, Harlan Ellison and Richard Matheson. Some great writers published books with Fawcett near the end of their careers such as Cornell Woolrich, David Goodis, Sax Rohmer, Lester Dent and W. R. Burnett, while others such as John D. MacDonald and Donald Hamilton spent their entire careers there.

The quotations are grouped by recurring themes or expressions, most of which are self-explanatory. At least one of the categories, however, needs an explanation. "A Sound of Distant Drums" is a collection of all the references to the aforementioned, often-used fictitious title of movies, plays and books in the novels of Donald Westlake and Lawrence Block. It became an inside joke between the two writers and sometimes included jibes at one another and even at themselves.

I first became aware of this on-going joke from Charles Ardai, the editor and publisher of Hard Case Crime. I noticed the "Sound of Distant Drums" title in books by both him and his partner, Max Phillips and a reference Max made to a title that also appeared in an Elizabeth McCracken novel; "Carter and Sharp on the High Seas." When I asked Charles about it, he told me the story about the joke between the two authors and how he and Max were paying homage to it by keeping it going.

As it turned out, the "Sound of Distant Drums" title appeared in three of the first four books under the Hard Case Crime imprint, Grifter's Game (a reprint of Mona) by Lawrence Block, Fade to Blonde by Max Phillips and Little Girl Lost by Richard Aleas (Charles Ardai).

In addition to Block's and Westlake's crime novels that use the Distant Drums title, I've also included the various sexploitation novels they wrote under various pseudonyms in which the title appears. It's the only category that has quotes from books other than crime novels.

J. V.

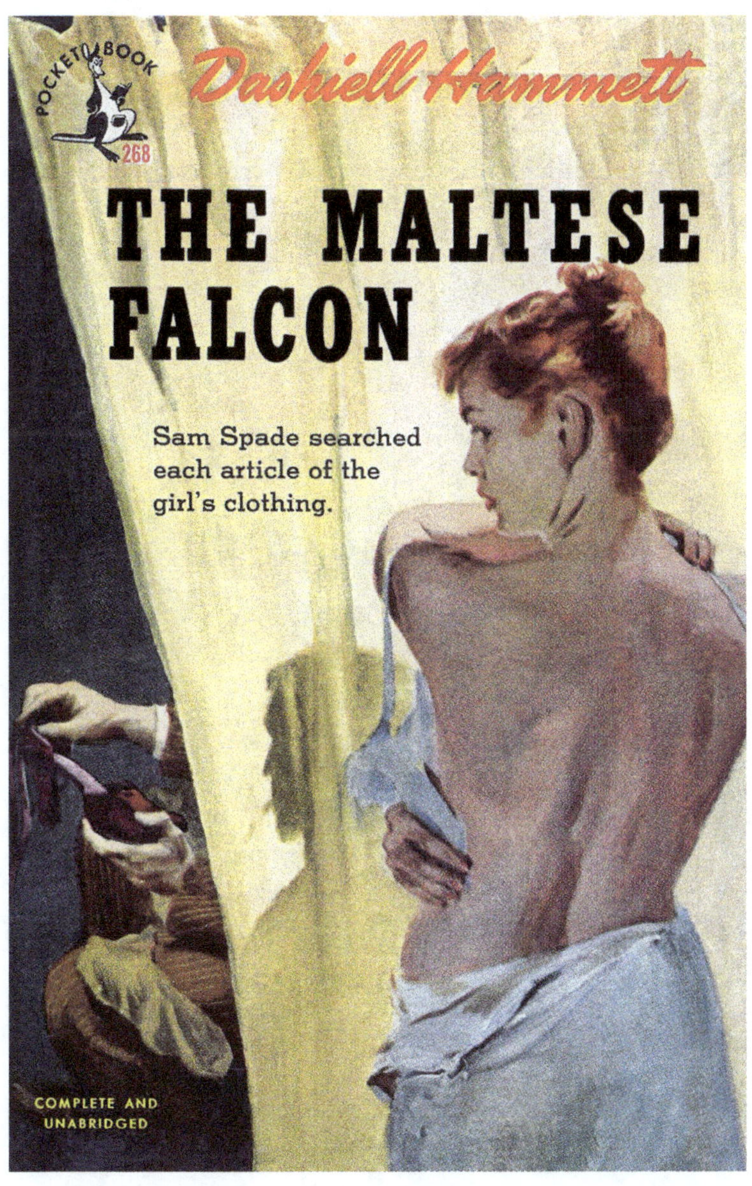
POCKET BOOK
268
Dashiell Hammett
THE MALTESE FALCON
Sam Spade searched each article of the girl's clothing.
COMPLETE AND UNABRIDGED

2696
POCKET BOOK
25¢
THE
COMPLETE
BOOK
POCKET
BOOKS
INC.
RAYMOND CHANDLER'S
THE BIG
SLEEP
A luscious
mantrap leads
Philip Marlowe to a
West Coast murder wave!

Pumping Lead

“What’s the rumpus?” I asked him.

He looked at me carefully before he replied, as if he wanted to be sure that the information was going into safe hands. His eyes were gray as his clothes, but not so soft.

“Don Willsson’s gone to sit on the right hand of God, if God don’t mind looking at bullet holes.”

“Who shot him?” I asked.

The gray man scratched the back of his neck and said: “Somebody with a gun.”

—Dashiell Hammett,
Red Harvest, 1927

The man in the derby hat raised his arm and Rico rushed him, pumping lead. Rico saw a long spurt of flame and then something hit him a sledge-hammer blow in the chest. He took two steps, dropped his gun, and fell flat on his face. He heard a rush of feet up the alley.

“Mother of God,” he said, “is this the end of Rico?”

—W. R. Burnett,
Little Caesar, 1929

The boy raised his eyes to Spade’s mouth and spoke in the strained voice of one in physical pain: “Keep on riding me and you’re going to be picking iron out of your navel.”

Spade chuckled. “The cheaper the crook, the gaudier the patter,” he said cheerfully.

—Dashiell Hammett,
The Maltese Falcon, 1930

After a while he stopped and turned and looked back and he could not see the light any more. Still he crawled on, dragged his torn body over the broken earth.

In the partial shelter of a steep sloping rock he stopped, sank forward, down.

There, after a little while, life went away from him.

—Paul Cain,
Fast One, 1933

Such a lot of guns around town and so few brains.

—Raymond Chandler,
The Big Sleep, 1939

"That gun of yours tickles me where I don't like to be tickled," she said.

—Jonathan Latimer,
The Fifth Grave, 1946

Be a good girl and put the gun away.

—George Harmon Coxe,
The Frightened Fiancée, 1950

Her face seemed to narrow and lengthen. I had never seen her look ugly before. An ugly woman with a gun is a terrible thing.

—Ross Macdonald,
The Way Some People Die, 1951

"I didn't put the finger on you," roared Gentry, his face purpling with anger. "Gurley jumped to that conclusion himself."

"And you left him believing it. Don't forget that if I wake up dead from lead poisoning tomorrow."

—Brett Halliday,
What Really Happened, 1952

I turned the knob. I gave the door a yank and stuck the gun in my visitor's face.

And Maddy Parson let out a small scream.

It took a few minutes to calm her down. "You were joking," she said uncertainly. "It was your idea of a gag. Well, it wasn't very funny. I could have had a heart attack. Is that thing loaded, Ed?"

"I hope so."

"You——"

—Lawrence Block,
Mona, 1961

It was wrong. It was like arresting the gun for murder.

—Ellery Queen,
The Player on the Other Side, 1963

Before crossing the sidewalk to his car, he stood for a moment in the doorway, casing the street, his gun in his hand. He didn't expect any gunplay. If what she had said was true, the gunmen would not be in sight. It was just a precaution. He had learned the hard way not to believe anybody entirely when it's your own life at stake.

—Chester Himes,
The Heat's On, 1966

He felt suddenly foolish again, innocent and foolish and unsuspecting. Her face was set and hard behind the barrel of the gun.

"Is that thing loaded?"

—John Lange (Michael Crichton),
Zero Cool, 1969

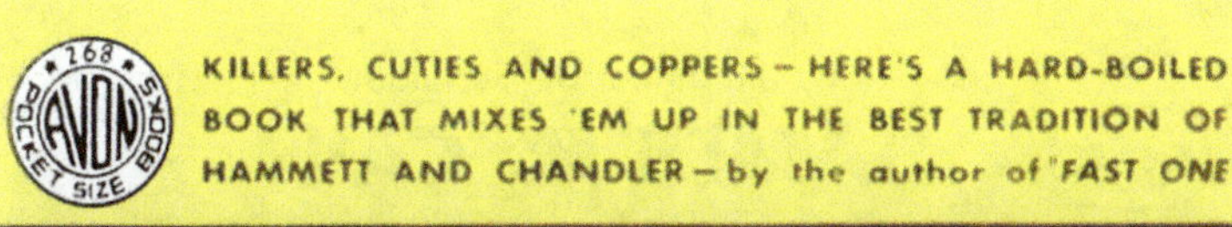
268
AVON
POCKET SIZE BOOKS
KILLERS, CUTIES AND COPPERS – HERE'S A HARD-BOILED BOOK THAT MIXES 'EM UP IN THE BEST TRADITION OF HAMMETT AND CHANDLER – by the author of "FAST ONE"
SEVEN SLAYERS
COMPLETE AND UNABRIDGED
PAUL CAIN

784

By the author of "Serenade"

JAMES M. CAIN

DOUBLE INDEMNITY

SIGNET BOOKS

Complete and Unabridged

Ugly Words Like Blackmail and Murder

"Blackmail is an ugly word," he says once.

"Not half so ugly as murder," retorts Gordon, and notes it with satisfaction in his diary.

Murder was the last word he wrote there.

—Mary Roberts Rinehart,
The Red Lamp, 1925

What real detecting had he done? None. His interest in Dimitrios had already become an obsession. 'Obsession' was an ugly word. It conjured up visions of bright, stupid eyes and proofs that the world was flat. Yet this business of Dimitrios did fascinate him and in an unaccountable way.

—Eric Ambler,
A Coffin for Dimitrios, 1939

"Have you forgotten last night already?" He whirled toward her. "Good God, is that all a murder means to you?"

"Murder is an ugly word." She tried to be coquettish with her eyelashes.

—Brett Halliday,
The Corpse Came Calling, 1942

Hilton looked at me oddly, and compressed his lips. "The sheriff is quite certain there has been a murder."

It was an ugly word. I had thought of it, Hilton and I together had thought of it without saying it, I had said it aloud to the night editor of The Press. But hearing it spoken—at me—so baldly I could feel the brutality that Hilton felt when he spoke. The shock went clear to my shoes.

—Louis Trimble,
Give Up the Body, 1946

I don't like to get mad like that. But I couldn't help it. Murder is an ugly word.

—Mickey Spillane,
My Gun is Quick, 1950

You handed me a jolt when I first saw you here. You handed me a jolt when you mentioned murder. It's an ugly word. But that's all there is to it. Go on. Run along. I'm getting tired of you already.

—Frederick Nebel,
Six Deadly Dames, 1950

It came to me in a rush that murder had begun to cling to me like so many leeches.

—A. S. Fleischman,
Malay Woman, 1954

“Is blackmail a new field for you?”

“Maiden voyage.”

“I must say you have a masterly grasp of its intricacies, for a beginner.”

“Thank you. I like your legs.”

“You don’t have any trouble with the moral aspects?”

“Why should I? I’m just a press agent in reverse. You’re paying me to keep you off the front page.”

The brown eyes met mine probingly. “Never mind the comic rationalization. It doesn’t bother you in the slightest, does it?”

“No. I’m a bastard. I admit it.”

—Charles Williams,
The Big Bite, 1956

Surely you wouldn’t be contemplating a sort of genteel blackmail, would you?” But blackmail was never genteel; however one dressed it up it was an ugly word.

—Robert Traver,
Anatomy of a Murder, 1958

591
NAL
SIGNET
BOOKS
By the author of "Serenade"
JAMES M. CAIN
MILDRED PIERCE
SIGNET BOOKS
Complete and Unabridged

10¢
WILLIAM IRISH
DELL
BOOK
11
A cheap and evil girl sets a
hopped-up killer against a city.
MARIHUANA
COMPLETE
AND
UNABRIDGED

80
PB
SHE WAS BEAUTIFUL AND VICIOUS – AND SHE WAS AFTER FIVE MEN!
Beware the Lady
(THE BRIDE WORE BLACK)
CORNELL WOOLRICH
COMPLETE AND UNABRIDGED
25c

Femmes Fatales

He remembered with growing indignation the calm manner in which Ann had sent him downstairs. Women were queer. They'd fuss over a man going out in a rainstorm or on a fishing trip, but they'd send him after a burglar as offhandedly as they would for the morning milk.

—Jonathan Latimer,
Red Gardenias, 1939

It was a blonde. A blonde to make a bishop kick a hole in a stained-glass window.

—Raymond Chandler,
Farewell, My Lovely, 1940

"Anytime I fall for a dame like you I hope that somebody will take me outside an' cut my head off quick because I would rather be tied up to a coupla wild alligators than get myself hitched on to you.

—Peter Cheyney,
Your Deal, My Lovely, 1941

That's the kind of dame that spends her life looking for trouble and when she finds it, it's the fault of the first guy she can get her fingernails into.

—Raymond Chandler,
The High Window, 1942

She was blonde as hell, wearing a lot of black.

—Kenneth Fearing,
The Big Clock, 1946

It seemed to me then that evil was a female quality, a poison that women secreted and transmitted to men like disease.

—Ross Macdonald,
The Moving Target, 1949

I'd read someplace that there was one woman like this for every man. One evil bitch, or not evil, but one that could scar your soul, shred it to a bloody pulp, just with a glance. With a thought, even. Snare, trap you, talk you into anything. One you'd do anything for, knowing you didn't even love her. Knowing it was only want, desire. One that could drive you into black madness, into a deathless, grinning glassy-eyed hell.

—Gil Brewer,
13 French Street, 1951

It was hot. It was dark. The cell block smelled of men sleeping with dreams. Men without women for years. Of fear and despair and frustration. Night after night, alone. Three walls, a high window, iron bars. A hard, narrow cot—and you. With disinfectant replacing affection. A small squirrel in a big cage. Staring hot-eyed into the dark. Wanting a drink. Wanting a woman. Trying not to blow your top. Hysteria building up inside you.

—Day Keene,
Hunt the Killer, 1951

She was in trouble, and she had passed it on to me like an infection and standing here in the rain I didn't give a damn.

—A. S. Fleischman,
Danger in Paradise, 1953

Sure, Fay could be a big help. Sure, she could make things a lot easier for me. So what? She could do something else, too. If she was smart enough to see it. Because how can you really trust a dame who'll help kill her own husband?

—Jim Thompson,
Savage Night, 1953

I got both hands on her throat and there was nothing inside me but the black madness of that desire to kill her, to close my hands until she turned purple and lay still and there'd be an end to her forever. Let them send me to the chair. Let 'em burn me. All they could do was kill me.

—Charles Williams,
Hell Hath No Fury, 1953

The apartment was on the ninth floor. I stood by the big windows in the living room and looked out over the bay. It was sparkling and clear in the morning sunshine, and I could see a boat going out to Alcatraz. They've got a view over there too, I thought, but they don't like it. A whole rock covered with tough guys and wisenheimers who knew more than the cops. And just beyond, out of sight up the bay, was San Quentin, where the state of California kept its smart characters who could never be caught. I remembered that awful minute in the hotel room in El Paso when I'd opened the door and seen her standing there with the two men in white Texas-sheriff hats. How many warnings did I need?

—Charles Williams,
Nothing in Her Way, 1953

I sat down in a booth, and the waitress shoved a menu in front of me. There wasn't anything on it that sounded good, and anyway, one look at her and my stomach turned flipflops... Every goddamned restaurant I go to, it's always the same way... They'll have some old bag on the payroll—I figure they keep her locked up in the mop closet until they see me coming. And they'll doll her up in the dirtiest goddamned apron they can find and smear that crappy red polish all over her fingernails, and everything about her is smeary and sloppy and smelly. And she's the dame that always waits on me.

—Jim Thompson,
A Hell of a Woman, 1954

Her name was Joyce Dugan, and at four o'clock on this February afternoon she had no remote thought that within the hour before closing time she was about to commit an act that would instigate a chain of murders.

—Frederic Brown,
His Name Was Death, 1954

I knew I'd never get enough of her. She was straight out of hell.

—Gil Brewer,
The Vengeful Virgin, 1958

She looked hot enough to catch fire, but too lazy to do anything but just lie there and smoke.

—Gil Brewer,
The Vengeful Virgin, 1958

She looked slick as all hell; polished, neat, and with that feminine deadliness that can drive you nuts. They work on it till they get complete control of the situation. There's no use trying to break them down then. They've made it.

She was like steel. It was in her eyes, and in her voice, and in the fine, shining look of her. From the sparkling ankles to the expensive-looking crink of a hat. She looked sexy and untouchable, the way they can look if they want. She looked expensive.

—Gil Brewer,
Nude on Thin Ice, 1960

I came at her like a bull at a matador and wrapped myself up in velvety skin. She made love with the freshness of an impatient virgin and the ingenuity of a sex-scarred whore. Her nails poked holes in my back and her thighs almost choked me.

—Lawrence Block,
Mona, 1961

She was trouble looking for somebody to happen to.

—Ross Macdonald,
The Wycherly Woman, 1961

I looked at the lovely and slightly soiled little blondie. I wondered what I would do with her if I really had the power to judge her and sentence her. Like the true eccentric, she thought she was just like everybody else. She was a cold mischief, with looks which had kept her from paying any penalties. In a small wind in the clearing, blowing toward me, she smelled of scent, of repellent, and a small sharp smell of nervous perspiration. She was too self-involved, in money hunger and pleasure hunger, to be the legendary femme fatale. She was a blunderer, but she would keep landing on her feet. She was never going to bring anyone any luck.

—John D. MacDonald,
A Deadly Shade of Gold, 1965

I had been emotionally involved a few times with women with enough of a record of promiscuity to make me vaguely uneasy. It is difficult to put much value on something the lady has distributed all too generously. I have the feeling there is some mysterious quota, which varies with each woman.

—John D. MacDonald,
Darker Than Amber, 1966

I turned up the air conditioning.

"That feels good," she said. Her presence beside me sustained an illusive feeling that there was an opening there into another time-track or dimension. It had more future than the world I knew, and not so bloody much traffic.

After I made the turn onto Sepulveda, I spent a little time preparing a remark.

"I seem to be getting less lonely, Mrs. Broadhurst."

"Call me Jean. Mrs. Broadhurst sounds like my mother-in-law."

—Ross Macdonald,
The Underground Man, 1971

LION
LIBRARY
35¢
"THE MOST TERRIFYING NOVEL OF THE SEASON"
—Detroit News
the bedside
CORPSE
originally published as THE GRAY EYES
STUART
FRIEDMAN
Sensual, sleek, deadly...
her name was Nora
LL 148

Lion Books
25¢
HER PROPOSITION WAS SIMPLE:
BE A CON WITH A NUMBER—
OR A CORPSE WITH A NAME
RECOIL
JIM THOMPSON
author of
A HELL OF A WOMAN
LB 124

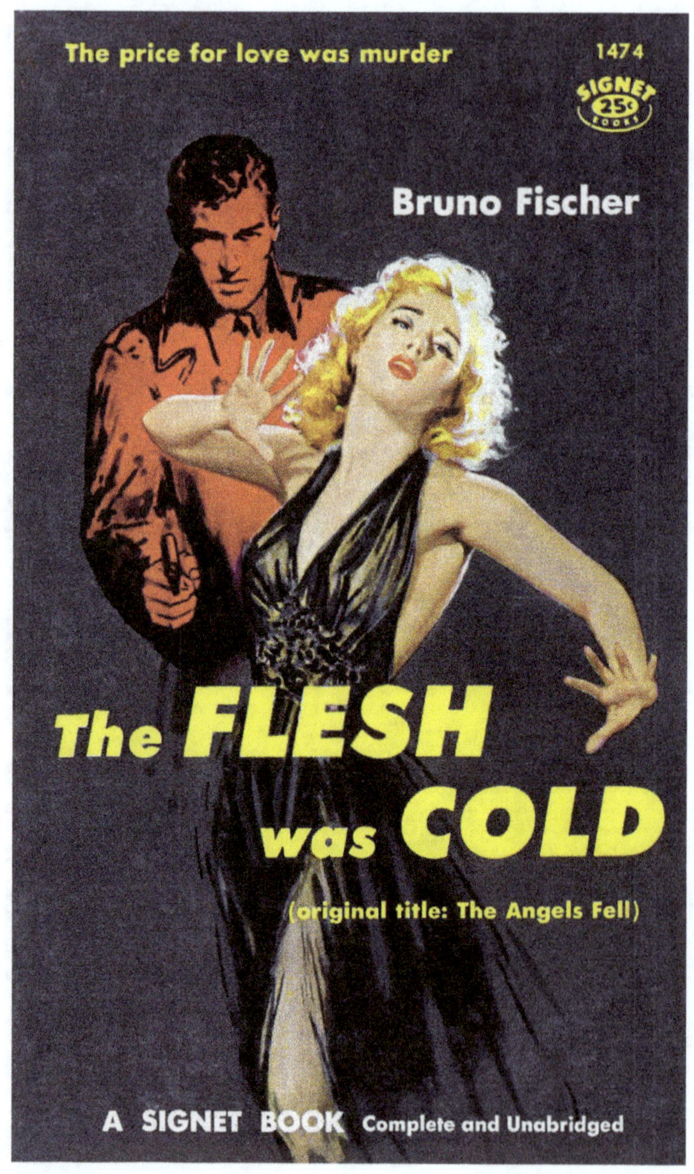
The price for love was murder
1474
SIGNET
25¢
BOOKS
Bruno Fischer
The FLESH was COLD
(original title: The Angels Fell)
A SIGNET BOOK Complete and Unabridged

Existential Angst

I first heard Personville called Poisonville by a red-haired mucker named Hickey Dewey in the Big Ship in Butte. He also called his shirt a shoit. I didn't think anything of what he had done to the city's name. Later I heard men who could manage their r's give it the same pronunciation. I still didn't see anything in it but the meaningless sort of humor that used to make richardsnary the thieves' word for dictionary. A few years later I went to Personville and learned better.

—Dashiell Hammett,
Red Harvest, 1927

He felt like somebody had taken the lid off life and let him look at the works.

—Dashiell Hammett,
The Maltese Falcon, 1927

There was a desert wind blowing that night. It was one of those hot, dry Santa Anas that come down through the mountain passes and curl your hair and make your nerves jump and your skin itch. On nights like that every booze party ends in a fight. Meek little wives feel the edge of the carving knife and study their husbands' necks. Anything can happen. You can even get a full glass of beer at a cocktail lounge.

—Raymond Chandler,
Red Wind, 1933

Everybody pays so much attention to living and so little to dying. Why are these high-powered scientists always screwing around trying to prolong life instead of finding pleasant ways to end it? There must be a hell of a lot of people in the world like me—who want to die but haven't got the guts.

—Horace McCoy,
They Shoot Horses, Don't They? 1935

Life is a ball game. You have to take a swing at whatever comes along before you wake up and find you've struck out

—Martin M. Goldsmith,
Detour, 1939

I keep trying to forget what happened—and I have, almost—except that once in a while, I wonder what might have taken place and what my life might have been if that damned grey roadster hadn't stopped. And when I start wondering, well, sometimes I want to curse and sometimes I want to cry.

Dramatics, buddy? No, sir. No dramatics. God or Fate or some mysterious force can put the finger on you or on me for no good reason at all.

—Martin M. Goldsmith,
Detour, 1939

There were three of them in the room now, where only two had first come in. Death was in the room with the two of them.

—William Irish (Cornell Woolrich),
Marihuana, 1941

Human beings shouldn't have to enter such doors, shouldn't have to stay behind them. No moon ever entered there, no stars, no anything at all. They were worse than the grave, for in the grave is an absence of consciousness. And god, she reflected, ordered the grave for all of us; but god didn't order such burrows in a third-rate New York City hotel.

—Cornell Woolrich,
Deadline at Dawn, 1944

There are things that have to be forgotten if you want to go on living.

—Jim Thompson,
The Killer Inside Me, 1952

When you stop growing you start dying.

—William Lee (William S. Burroughs),
Junkie, 1953

The darkness and myself. Everything else was gone. And the little that was left of me was going, faster and faster.

—Jim Thompson,
Savage Night, 1953

After all, no matter how long you live, there aren't too many really delicious moments along the way, since most of life is spent eating and sleeping and waiting for something to happen that never does. You can figure it up for yourself, using your own life as the scoreboard. Most of living is waiting to live. And you spend a great deal of time worrying about things that don't matter and about people that don't matter and all this is clear to you when you know the very day you're going to die.

—Elliott Chaze,
Black Wings Has My Angel, 1953

He was dignity distorted, bravery become knavery, sanctimoniousness masking sin. He was a mirror, jeering at the subject it reflected. Yet so muted were the jeers, so delicate the inaccuracies of delineation, that they evaded detection. True and false were blended together. The false was merely an extended shadow of the true.

—Jim Thompson,
A Swell-Looking Babe, 1954

The phone rang. Softly, in actuality, yet it seemed loud and ominous, as phones do at night in dark hotel rooms.

—Jim Thompson,
The Nothing Man, 1954

What sense does it all make? What sort of God would put us here in this goddamned, stinking slaughterhouse of a world? Some guy that likes to tear the wings off flies? What use is there in living and starving and fighting the next guy for a full belly? It's a nut house.

—William Lindsay Gresham,
Nightmare Alley, 1956

I felt as out of place as a blind man at a burlesque show.

—W. R. Burnett,
It's Always Four O'Clock, 1956

He stayed there, kneeling as though in fervent supplication. Then very slowly he shook his head, sadly refusing the supplicant. As he got to his feet, it seemed he was falling instead of rising. There was a certain dullness in his eyes, a certain look that said, it's the escalator going down and where it stops don't matter.

—David Goodis,
Fire in the Flesh, 1957

Doom. You recognize Doom easily. It's a feeling and a taste, and it's black, and it's very heavy. It comes down over your head, and wraps tentacles around you, and sinks long dirty fingernails into your heart. It has a stink of burning garbage.

—Gil Brewer,
The Vengeful Virgin, 1958

The sky was dirty. A slow wind came in across Tampa Bay, like the hot breath of an eager woman.

—Gil Brewer,
Wild, 1958

There was a sense of doom. It was something you couldn't read, couldn't decipher. Too much, I thought, not knowing what "too much" meant. It was as if the place held its breath. It was crazy, maybe like that moment just before the explosion when the nightmared gymnast is shot from the circus cannon. What did he feel at that moment?

—Gil Brewer,
Nude on Thin Ice, 1960

Nothing was true but the fatigue of life and the eternal disappointment.

— Patricia Highsmith,
This Sweet Sickness, 1960

I think death will come like that, in the form of a person. When you meet that person or see him or her, I think you'll know it, because it'll have something very close to do with you.

—Patricia Highsmith,
The Cry of the Owl, 1962

"You won't make it, Keith," she said. A great sadness was in her voice.

The sadness reached out and touched him. Almost he let it go through. But then he forced himself to laugh. "Why not? Other cats have made it."

"But not you, Keith. Even if you were within reach of it, you wouldn't let yourself stretch that last inch."

"So what's the diff, a hundred years from now?"

"No difference a hundred years from now. But we don't have a hundred years. The difference is today and tomorrow."

She was so right that a sense of doom overwhelmed him. It had lain buried in him all his life. He recognized it now. He had glimpsed it before, many times, in a dream, or in his father's eyes. At last he was face to face with it, and the face of doom was no stranger.

—Ellery Queen,
Beware the Young Stranger, 1965

He didn't ask for excuses, he didn't give any. As far as he was concerned, the world was a shitpot with a barbed-wire handle and the further he could kick it the better he liked it. As far as he was concerned, he had plenty owing to him. And he was hell on wheels at collecting.

—Jim Thompson,
Texas by the Tail, 1965

"The life is its own reward," I countered. "I like to move into people's lives and then move out again.

Living with one set of people in one place used to bore me."

"That isn't your real motivation. I know your type. You have a secret passion for justice. Why don't you admit it?"

"I have a secret passion for mercy," I said. "But justice is what keeps happening to people."

—Ross Macdonald,
The Goodbye Look, 1969

Does one exist, or to what extent does one exist as an individual without friends, family, anybody to whom one can relate, to whom one's existence is of the least importance?

—Patricia Highsmith,
The Tremor of Forgery, 1969

127
Meet Shell Scott, Fast with Gun or Gal
Fast with the Answer for Murder, Too...
GOLD MEDAL BOOK
CASE OF THE
VANISHING BEAUTY
Richard S. Prather

423
GOLD MEDAL BOOK
THE AVENGER returns—to track down the world's most dangerous beauty
DEATH IS A LOVELY DAME
©

25¢
Matthew Blood

Drinking, Smoking & Other Vices

"I don't see what there is to be cagey about," she snapped. "And I don't like your manners."

"I'm not crazy about yours," I said. "I didn't ask to see you. You sent for me. I don't mind your ritzing me or drinking your lunch out of a Scotch bottle. I don't mind your showing me your legs. They're very swell legs and it's a pleasure to make their acquaintance. I don't mind if you don't like my manners. They're pretty bad. I grieve over them during the long winter evenings. But don't waste your time trying to cross-examine me."

—Raymond Chandler,
The Big Sleep, 1939

I got up on my feet and went over to the bowl in the corner and threw cold water on my face. After a little while I felt a little better, but very little. I needed a drink, I needed a lot of life insurance, I needed a vacation, I needed a home in the country. What I had was a coat, a hat and a gun. I put them on and went out of the room.

—Raymond Chandler,
Farewell, My Lovely, 1940

The lights of the city streaked off below him like the luminous spokes of a warped wheel. An indistinctly outlined, pearly moon seemed to drip down the sky, like a clot of incandescent tapioca thrown up against the night by a cosmic comic. He lit the after-the-dance, while-waiting-for-her-to-come-back cigarette

—Cornell Woolrich,
The Bride Wore Black, 1940

He had met him before, that certain down-at-heel vet growing stooped from carrying a thirty-five-pound monkey on his back.

—Nelson Algren,
The Man With the Golden Arm, 1949

"Alcohol is like love," he said. "The first kiss is magic, the second is intimate, the third is routine. After that you take the girl's clothes off."

—Raymond Chandler,
The Long Goodbye, 1953

Parnell, as always, took his whisky straight and followed it with a quick gulp of water. For a man suffering from chronic arthritis, and a little drunk, too, I thought the movements were incredibly swift and dexterous. But then, I reflected, the man had had years and years of practice. Practice, in fact, was Parnell's big trouble. For here was probably the smartest lawyer I ever knew, both the smartest and least successful.

—Robert Traver,
Anatomy of a Murder, 1958

At the tavern, he pushed inside through a heavy plate-glass door and advanced on a redfaced Irishman behind the horseshoe bar. Mickey Tallant was a beefy man with short, thick arms and big-knuckled sledgehammers attached to the ends of them. He had no hair at all, a ravaged kewpie-doll face, and a cauliflower ear. A damp white towel encircled his ample girth.

—Dan Marlowe,
Shake a Crooked Town, 1961

"Looking for someone?" she said.

"Just waiting."

"For Lefty or for Godot? It makes a difference."

"For Lefty Godot. The pitcher."

"The pitcher in the rye?"

"He prefers bourbon."

"So do I," she said. "You sound like an anti-intellectual to me, Mr.—"

"Archer. Didn't I pass the test?"

"It depends on who does the grading."

—Ross Macdonald,
The Chill, 1963

When I finally caught up with Abraham Trahearne, he was drinking beer with an alcoholic bulldog named Fireball Roberts in a ramshackle joint outside of Sonoma, California, drinking the heart right out of a fine spring afternoon.

—James Crumley,
The Last Good Kiss, 1978

CREST BOOK
173
25¢
She was jail bait with an angel's face—
but he couldn't leave her alone
Little Tramp
GIL BREWER
By the author of — AND THE GIRL SCREAMED

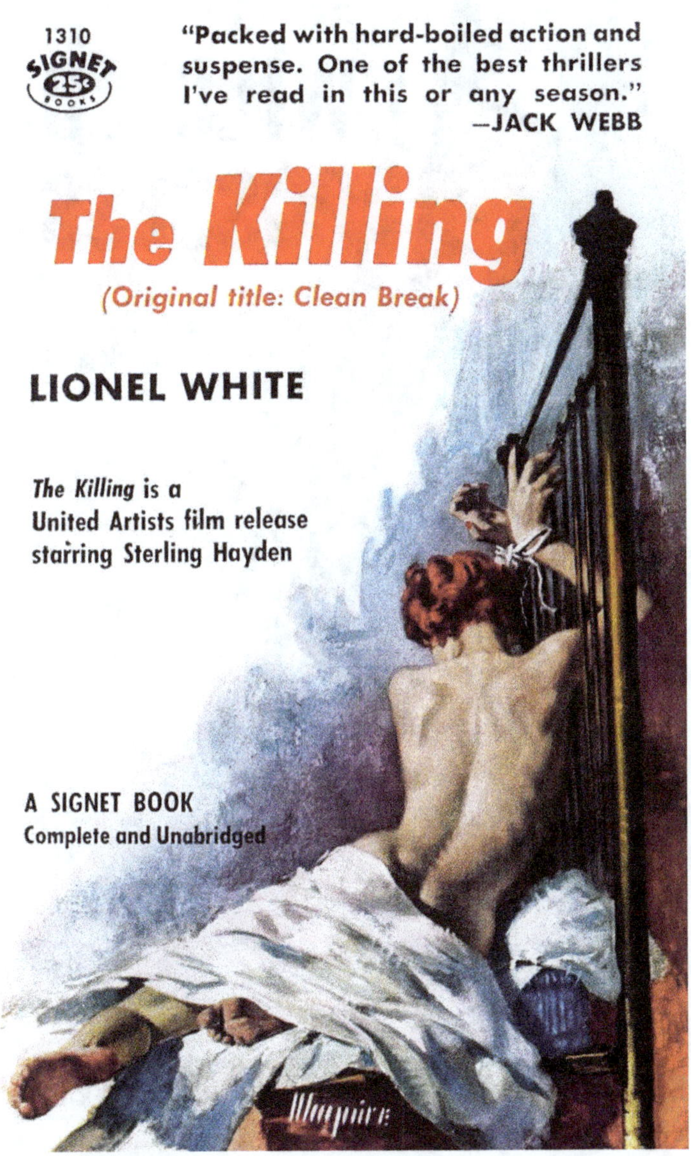

1310

"Packed with hard-boiled action and suspense. One of the best thrillers I've read in this or any season."
—JACK WEBB

The Killing

(Original title: Clean Break)

LIONEL WHITE

The Killing **is a United Artists film release starring Sterling Hayden**

A SIGNET BOOK
Complete and Unabridged

364
MONARCH
BOOKS
40c
WILD TO
POSSESS
She Lit A Fuse
Inside Men
GIL BREWER

I Like Women Warm to the Touch

"She's a nice girl. Not my type."

"You don't like them nice?" He had another cigarette going. The smoke was being fanned away from his face by his hand.

"I like smooth shiny girls, hardboiled and loaded with sin."

"They take you to the cleaners," Randall said indifferently.

"Sure. Where else have I ever been? What do you call this session?"

—Raymond Chandler,
Farewell, My Lovely, 1940

I like women who swoon at the sight of firearms and tremble at shadows.

—Richard Powell,
Shoot If You Must, 1946

I like my women warm to the touch. And not quite so deadly with a gun.

—Charles Williams,
A Touch of Death, 1953

I like women big, something you can get a grip on. I don't go for this skimpy stuff.

—Chandler Brossard,
The Bold Saboteurs, 1953

She was a damned attractive woman, a little heavy in the thighs, perhaps, but I didn't consider that a detriment. I like women a little on the fleshy side. Skinny, boyish-type figures may be admired by other women, but not by most men.

—Charles Willeford,
Cockfighter, 1962

LION
A MARRIED WOMAN PLUNGES
TO THE MOST SINFUL DEPTHS
25c
ALLEY GIRL
JONATHAN CRAIG
A LION
ORIGINAL
206

SUGAR

She had a child's face,
a woman's body—and the
key to a quarter
of a million bucks

By Gil Brewer
author of LITTLE TRAMP
and WILD

An Avon Original 35c—T335

A Ticket to the Gas Chamber

A tingle ran up my spine and I was aware of a feeling of suppressed excitement and I knew I'd have to step carefully. This could be either a ticket to the gas chamber or the means of collecting a lot of dough. It depended how I played it.

—James Hadley Chase,
You Never Know With Women, 1949

At the moment you don't realize that you're taking the first step toward the gas chamber; you're not thinking a thing except that you're hooked and you might as well get it off your chest. Any veteran cop can give you examples by the dozen. It's usually a case of the right word at the right time.

—Octavious Roy Cohen,
Lost Lady, 1951

"I read once that this man was in the chair and when the electrocutioner threw the switch the smoke came out of the man's head and formed a question mark over him and everybody said it was an omen, that maybe he didn't commit the murder they killed him for."

"Well," I said, "if they catch me, there won't be any question mark. There'll be an exclamation point."

—Elliott Chaze,
Black Wings Has My Angel, 1953

It'll be a damned shame and a waste of raw material if they put that big, beautiful body of yours in the gas chamber, but you're like so many murderers, Belle. You just can't leave well enough alone.

—Brett Halliday,
Pay-Off in Blood, 1962

296
GOLD MEDAL BOOK
She had the face of a madonna
and a heart made of dollar bills
BLACK WINGS
HAS MY ANGEL
ELLIOTT CHAZE
Original Gold Medal Novel—Not a Reprint

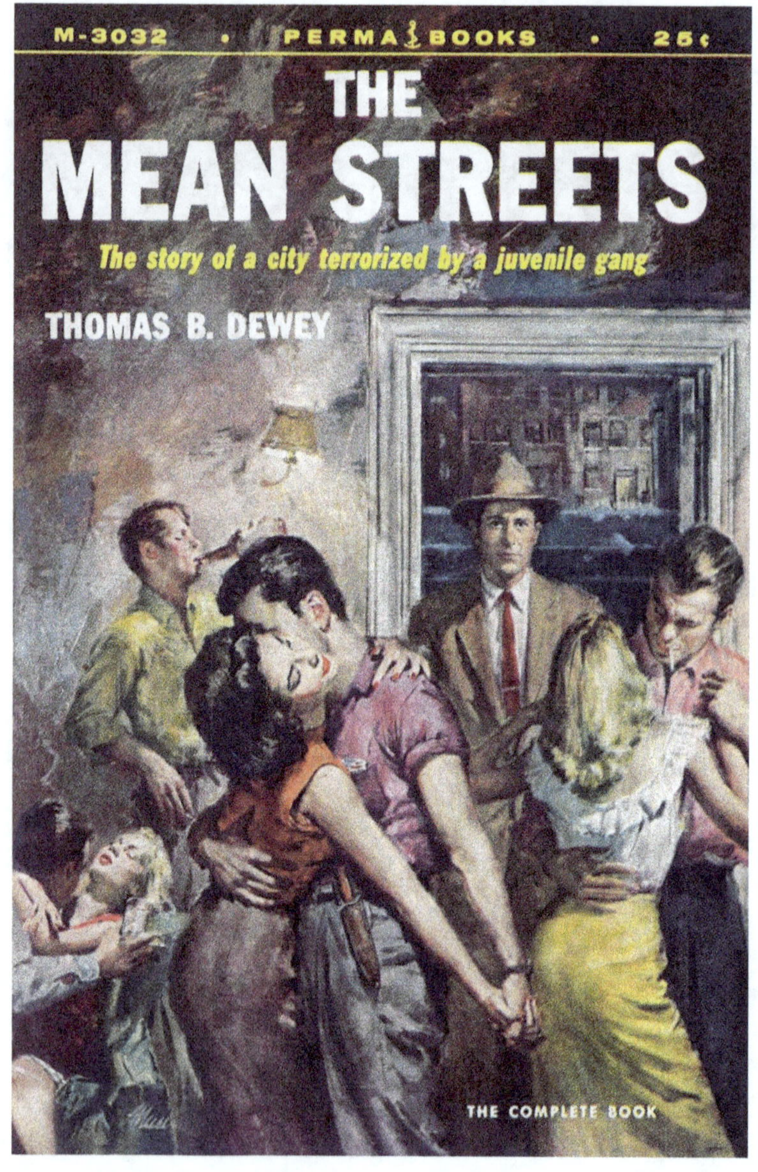
M-3032 • PERMA BOOKS • 25¢
THE
MEAN STREETS
The story of a city terrorized by a juvenile gang
THOMAS B. DEWEY
THE COMPLETE BOOK

Down These Mean Streets

You don't know what it means... You deal in arrests, to you it's nothing. You can't possibly know what goes through you, when you're in your room, secure and contented and at peace with the world one minute, and the next someone suddenly comes for you to take you away. Takes you down through the building you live in, in front of everybody, takes you through the streets—and when they get you there you find out you're supposed to have—to have murdered a man! Oh, I can't stand it! I'm frightened of the whole world tonight.

—Cornell Woolrich,
The Bride Wore Black, 1940

Down these mean streets a man must go who is not himself mean, who is neither tarnished nor afraid. He is the hero; he is everything. He must be a complete man and a common man and yet an unusual man. He must be, to use a rather weathered phrase, a man of honor—by instinct, by inevitability, without thought of it, and certainly without saying it. He must be the best man in his world and a good enough man for any world.

—Raymond Chandler,
The Simple Art of Murder, 1950

Winter was gray and mean upon the city and every night was a package of cold bleak hours, like the hours in a cell that had no door.

—David Goodis,
Of Tender Sin, 1952

Vern took another sip of his drink. He turned and looked through the glass of the door. The street gleamed wet in the night rain, and green neon across the street was reflected against the shiny black. It was a night to nurse a drink. It was a night to sit and feel a funny knot in your middle. This thing had, all at once, got out of hand.

—John D. MacDonald,
The Neon Jungle, 1953

Night and the rain had come back to New York, the air musty with dust driven up by the sudden surge of the downpour. The bars were filled, the sheltered areas under marquees crowded and an empty taxi a rare treasure to be fought over.

But it was a night to think in. There is a peculiar anonymity you can enjoy in the city on a rainy night. You're alone, yet not alone. The other people around you are merely motion and sound and the sign of life whose presence averts the panic of being truly alone, yet who observe the rules of the city and stay withdrawn and far away when they are close.

—Mickey Spillane,
The Girl Hunters, 1962

Bunny went through the front door in a sliding skid. The kid took one look at my face and started to run back around the front of the Olds. Across the street something went ker-blam! The kid whinnied like a horse with the colic. He ran in a circle for three seconds and then fell down in front of the Olds, his white cotton gloves in the dirty street and his legs still on the sidewalk. The left side of his head was gone.

—Dan Marlowe,
The Name of the Game is Death, 1962

This was the neighborhood of the cheap addicts, whisky-heads, stumblebums, the flotsam of Harlem; the end of the line for the whores, the hard squeeze for the poor honest laborers and a breeding ground for crime.

—Chester Himes,
Cotton Comes to Harlem, 1965

D311

"The Best Mystery of the Year"
—MYSTERY WRITERS OF AMERICA

35¢

A story about the special world of a private detective

By STANLEY ELLIN

The Eighth Circle

247
GOLD MEDAL BOOK
He was stretched on the rack of a corrupt and alien love
Cry at Dusk
LESTER DENT
AN ORIGINAL NOVEL—NOT A REPRINT ©

s1132
35¢
GOLD MEDAL BOOK
FREDRIC BROWN
MADBALL
Step right up, gents—
They're all alive inside.
Here's the sizzling classic
of carny life by the
celebrated author of
The Fabulous Clipjoint,
The Screaming Mimi, etc.
Mitchell Hooks

Never Trust a Man Who Doesn't Drink

I distrust a close-mouthed man. He generally picks the wrong time to talk and says the wrong things. Talking's something you can't do judiciously unless you keep in practice.

—Dashiell Hammett,
The Maltese Falcon, 1930

Never play cards with a man called Doc. Never eat at a place called Mom's. Never sleep with a woman whose troubles are worse than your own.

—Nelson Algren,
A Walk on the Wild Side, 1956

"Tough break," he said. "And all because of a—dumb broad—never trust a dame"

—Hartley Howard,
The Long Night, 1957

Bess was probably schitzy, I told myself, or addled on bedroom novels, suffering from cabin fever or faculty-wife neurosis or the first untimely hint of middle age, like frost on the Fourth of July. Clearly she had troubles, and a wise man I knew in Chicago had said once and for all: "Never sleep with anyone whose troubles are worse than your own."

—Ross Macdonald,
Black Money, 1966

A girl should never never never have an affair with the man she works for. It's such a stupid thing to do. It always has to end, you know, and then there's the terrible awkwardness of trying to work smoothly together, and usually the man gets rid of the secretary somehow.

—John D. MacDonald,
Nightmare in Pink, 1964

Never go to bed with a woman who has more troubles than you do.

—James Crumley,
The Wrong Case, 1975

"Son," he said without preamble, "never trust a man who doesn't drink because he's probably a self-righteous sort, a man who thinks he knows right from wrong all the time. Some of them are good men, but in the name of goodness, they cause most of the suffering in the world. They're the judges, the meddlers. And, son, never trust a man who drinks but refuses to get drunk. They're usually afraid of something down deep inside, either that they're a coward or a fool or mean and violent. You can't trust a man who's afraid of himself. But sometimes, son, you can trust a man who occasionally kneels before a toilet. The chances are that he is learning something about humility and his natural human foolishness, about how to survive himself. It's damned hard for a man to take himself too seriously when he's heaving his guts into a dirty toilet bowl."

—James Crumley,
The Wrong Case, 1975

CREST BOOK
349
25c
She made him forget
he was a cop
because she never
let him forget
he was a man
Devil in Dungarees
ALBERT CONROY
Author of MURDER IN ROOM 13

25c
GOLD MEDAL BOOK
JONATHAN CRAIG
SO YOUNG, SO WICKED
By the author of
CASE OF THE VILLAGE TRAMP
Meet Leda, the
dainty town beauty,
15 years old and getting
her kicks out of
grown men and
hot-blooded murder

Tough Guys with Ugly Mugs

The blonde behind the barrier was leaning forward with her neck craned, watching. She looked at him with open admiration. 'A real tough guy,' she said softly.

'Sure, baby,' Fenner returned, not pausing in his walk, 'but I could be mighty soft with a honey like you.'

—James Hadley Chase,
No Orchids for Miss Blandish, 1939

Dead men are heavier than broken hearts.

—Raymond Chandler,
The Big Sleep, 1939

You're a tough guy. Six feet of iron man. One hundred and ninety pounds stripped and with your face washed. Hard muscles and no glass jaw. You can take it. You've been sapped down twice, had your throat choked and been beaten half silly on the jaw with a gun barrel. You've been shot full of hop and kept under it until you're as crazy as two waltzing mice. And what does all that amount to? Routine.

—Raymond Chandler,
Farewell, My Lovely, 1940

"You know, I don't know if anybody's ever told you, but you're a heel."

"Maybe," I tell her. "Do I haveta weep because you think so?"

—Peter Cheyney,
You Can Always Duck, 1943

"Well, whenever it gets too bad, I just step out and kill a few people. I frig them to death with a barbed-wire cob I have. After that I feel fine."

I'd been trying to place him, and finally it had come to me. It'd been several years since I'd seen that big ugly mug in one of the out-of-town papers, and the picture hadn't been so good a resemblance. But I remembered it, now, and some of the story I'd read about him. He'd taken his degree at the University of Edinburgh at a time when we were admitting their graduates to practice. He'd killed half a dozen people before he picked up a jerkwater Ph.D., and edged into psychiatry.

—Jim Thompson,
The Killer Inside Me, 1952

Hagen went on hammering with his fists until there was nothing left to hammer. He pulled himself off the corpse and took out a handkerchief and stood there wiping the blood from his knuckles. Then he let the handkerchief fall onto the cot. It landed on the chest of the corpse. Some blood dropped off the edge of it, and sprinkled the hand of the corpse, the red drops glimmering on the dark fingers that still seemed to be groping for the blackjack.

—David Goodis,
Street of the Lost, 1952

He wondered if he was strong enough and quick enough to choke her to death without her being able to scream, here and now, beside her. He glanced sidewise at her, at her neck, thinking the move out, weighing the chances of being able to do it silently.

—Fredric Brown,
Madball, 1953

You see a boxer with a beautiful nose and you got a fighter without heart.

—Peter Rabe,
Kill the Boss Goodbye, 1956

"Now just a minute, shamus," Donovan said, starting up.

"Sit down," I said. "I've always wanted a picture of you to hang over my garbage can."

"What about your own ugly mug?"

"We'll tear it in two," I said. "You can have half."

—Thomas B. Dewey,
The Case of the Murdered Model, 1959

When the bandages came off, Parker looked in the mirror at a stranger.

—Richard Stark,
The Man with the Getaway Face, 1963

When you see the ugliness behind the tears of another person, it makes you take a closer look at your own.

—John D. MacDonald,
The Green Ripper, 1964

Some men spend their lives looking for ways to punish themselves for having been born, and Begley had some of the stigmata of the trouble-prone.

—Ross Macdonald,
The Chill, 1963

All men had these weaknesses in one form or another ... and their derelictions and failures were invariably the result of them. In other words, men were only rational by fits and starts. That was what was meant by human, all too human; and that was why the prisons were full ...

—W. R. Burnett,
The Asphalt Jungle, 1949

I got a theory a person ought to do everything it's possible to do before he dies, and maybe die trying to do something that's really impossible.

—Patricia Highsmith,
Strangers on a Train, 1950

209
GOLD MEDAL BOOK
Good girl or bad girl, was she worth the professor's life and reputation?
Fools Walk In
BRUNO FISCHER
AN ORIGINAL NOVEL—NOT A REPRINT ©

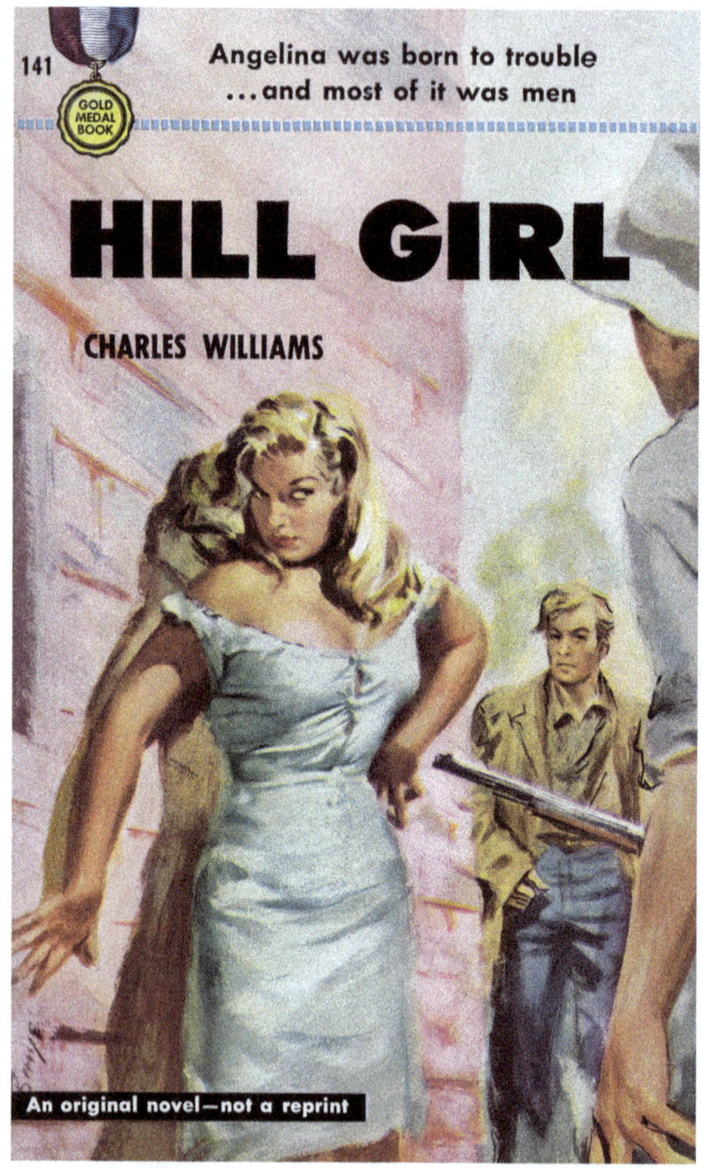
141
GOLD MEDAL BOOK
Angelina was born to trouble
...and most of it was men
HILL GIRL
CHARLES WILLIAMS
An original novel—not a reprint

Dirty Money

I stared into the darkness some more that night. I had killed a man, for money and a woman. I didn't have the money and I didn't have the woman. The woman was a killer, out-and-out, and she had made a fool of me.

—James M. Cain,
Double Indemnity, 1943

"There's a contradiction in your thinking," I said. "If I took your dirty money, you wouldn't be able to trust my honesty."

—Ross Macdonald,
The Drowning Pool, 1950

When a rich man dies it is more complex than when a poor man dies. A rich man doesn't simply quit living. He quits being rich, too.

—Elliott Chaze,
Black Wings Has My Angel, 1953

You remember that night in the Garden? You came down to the dressing room and said, 'Kid, this aint your night. We're goin' for the price on Wilson.' You remember that? This aint your night. My night! I could've taken Wilson apart that night. So what happens? He gets the title shot, outdoors in the ball park. And what do I get? A one-way ticket to Palookaville. I was never no good after that night. You remember that, Charley. It's like a—peak you reach, and then it's all downhill. It was you, Charley. You was my brother. You should've looked out for me a little bit. You should've taken care of me. Just a little bit. Instead of makin' me take them dives for the short-end money.

—Budd Schulberg,
On the Waterfront, 1955

Money is the root of all goodness. To talk disparagingly about money is the privilege of those who have money. There are also those people who state matter-of-factly that "money isn't everything". This statement is also true, but only so long as one has money.

—Charles Willeford,
Honey Gal, 1955

I'm on the make. Nothing matters in this goddamned lunatic asylum of a world but dough. When you get that you're the boss. If you don't have it you're the end man on the daisy chain. I'm going to get it if I have to bust every bone in my head doing it. I'm going to milk it out of those chumps and take them for the gold in their teeth before I'm through.

—William Lindsay Gresham,
Nightmare Alley, 1956

Oh, she'd got away with murder, and she had Lloyd's hidden money. But she had walked into hell: the hell of frustration. The kind of frustration that drove you insane. You knew what you wanted, you had it right with you, but it was rotten in the middle. It was no good. It was desire and excitement and sweet agony and it was always frustrated.

—Harry Whittington,
Fires That Destroy, 1958

The cross-eyed gods of the universal cash registers had punched the No Sale key, and the drawer was wide open—waiting. All I had to do was reach in and take the money and fill my pockets.

—Gil Brewer,
Nude on Thin Ice, 1960

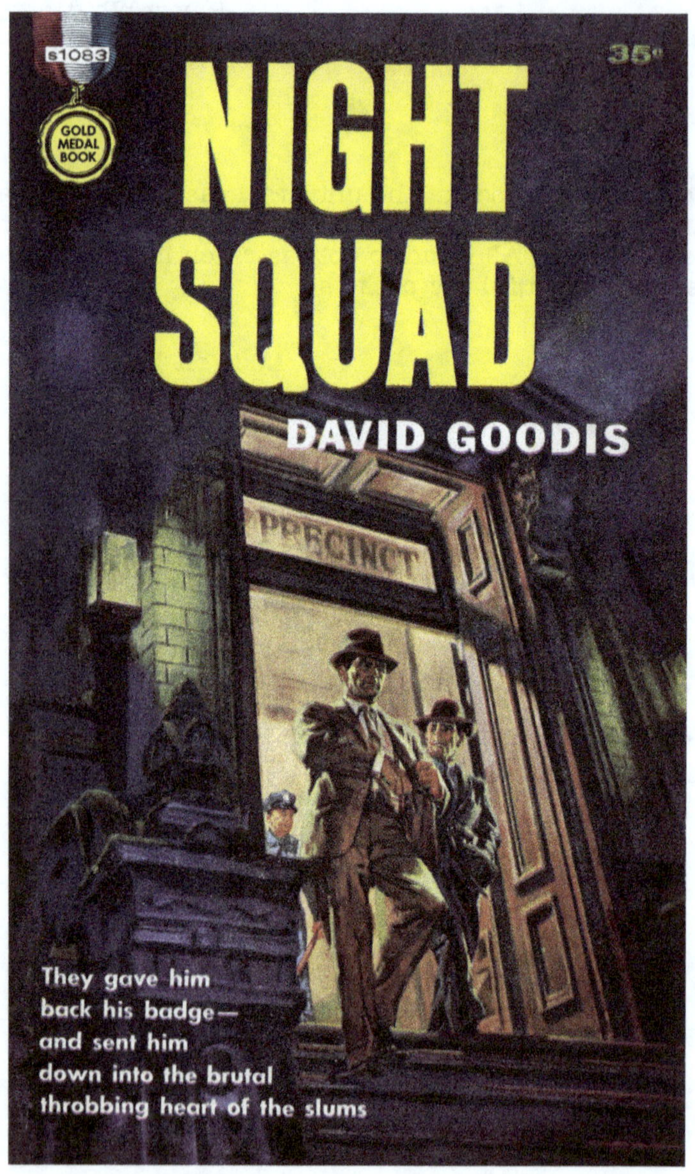
s1083
GOLD MEDAL BOOK
35¢
NIGHT SQUAD
DAVID GOODIS
PRECINCT
They gave him
back his badge—
and sent him
down into the brutal
throbbing heart of the slums

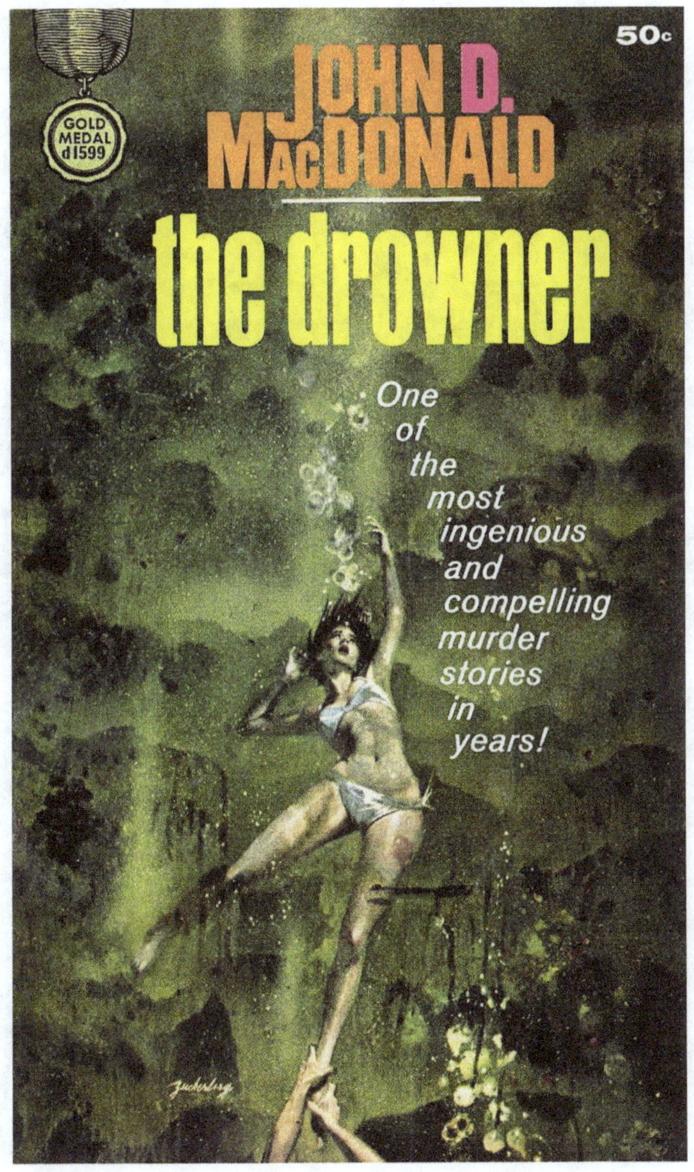
50c
GOLD
MEDAL
d1599
JOHN D.
MacDONALD
the drowner
One
of
the
most
ingenious
and
compelling
murder
stories
in
years!

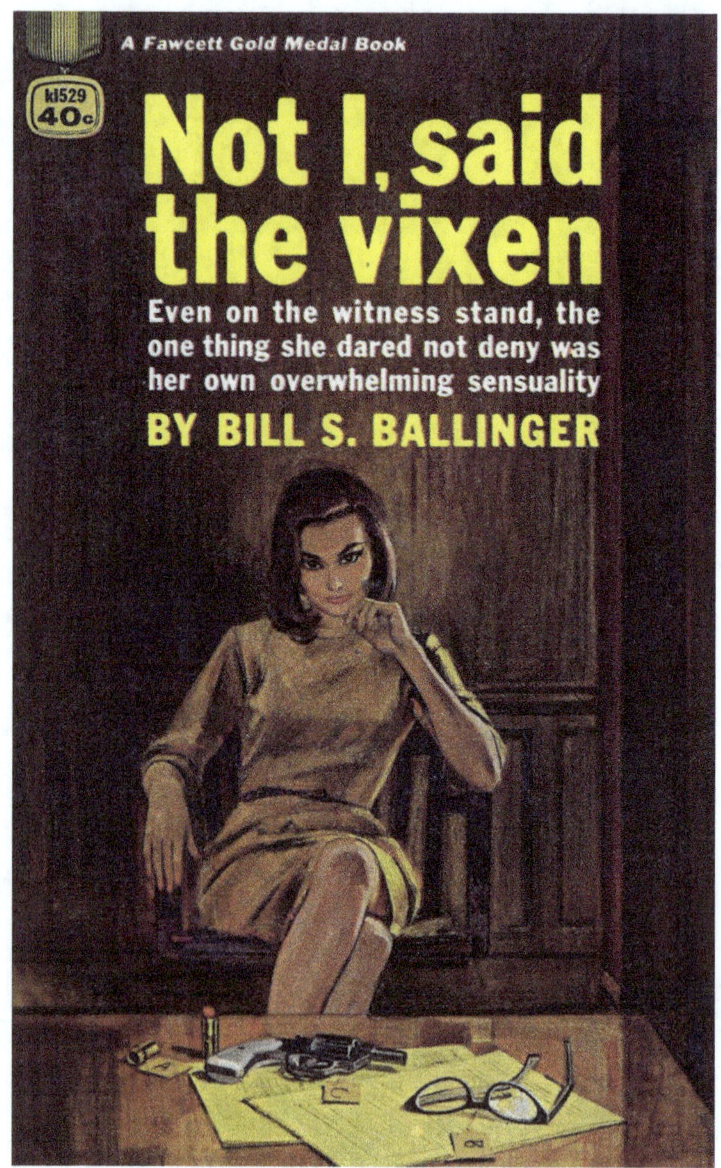
A Fawcett Gold Medal Book
k1529
40c
Not I, said the vixen
Even on the witness stand, the one thing she dared not deny was her own overwhelming sensuality
BY BILL S. BALLINGER

Just Pull the Trigger

"I've never fired one of these things, you know."

"It is easy. You release the safety catch, point it, pull the trigger and hope for the best."

—Eric Ambler,
Journey into Fear, 1940

I thought a minute, then took my gun from its holster. "Here. You know how to use this?"

She took it in her hand and gave it a look of obvious distaste. "Just pull the trigger thing, don't you?"

I groaned. "Yeah, you pull the trigger thing. But you don't have to pull that one very hard, so be damn careful how you handle it. And there's no safety on that gun." I let her look some more, then I said, "You simply point it at the man and pull the trigger. It makes a noise and he falls down."

—Richard S. Prather,
The Way of a Wanton, 1952

Now this is fully loaded, safety off. You pull this hammer back and then all you do is squeeze the trigger.

—Robert Colby,
Murder Mistress, 1959

Give me a double-action revolver every time. You can cock the hammer for a sighted shot, but you don't have to cock it; for a quick shot just pull the trigger and it goes bang. Every time, for six times. If you haven't hit what you're shooting at by then you had no business shooting at it in the first place.

—Fredric Brown,
Five Day Nightmare, 1962

Maybe you won't have to shoot anybody. If you do, just point the gun at the person you want to shoot. And squeeze the trigger.

—Lawrence Block,
Tanner's Tigers, 1968

226
GOLD MEDAL BOOK
He sought in strange places
childhood's haunting love
Of Tender Sin
David
Goodis
AN ORIGINAL NOVEL—NOT A REPRINT

s1074
GOLD MEDAL BOOK
35¢
VIN PACKER
THE DAMNATION OF ADAM BLESSING
Nowhere was there another man like him, a man who could march down the road to hell and find it paved with glory

Better Off Dead

Dollar for dollar paid down, there's a bigger face coverage on accident than any other kind. And it's the one kind of insurance that can be taken out without the insured knowing a thing about it. No physical examination for accident. On that, all they want is the money, and there's many a man walking around today that's worth more to his loved ones dead than alive, only he don't know it yet.

—James M. Cain,
Double Indemnity, 1936

This man would be better off dead. Why do we think death is so cruel? It's life that is cruel.

—Cornell Woolrich,
The Black Angel, 1943

I'm glad he's dead. All I want to do is prove it. I don't give a damn about Deke, or what happened to him. He's better off dead, for all concerned.

—Gil Brewer,
Wild to Possess, 1959

And all the while, below the dark and violent surface of the battle against the river and a disaster that could be recognized as such and fought against with weapons he could hold in his hands, there ran the apprehensive undercurrent of his fear for Jessie. She can't go away with that no-good slut, he thought. She just can't. She'd be safer with a rattlesnake. She'd be better off dead.

—Charles Williams,
Big City Girl, 1951

I want you to promise me that you won't take this the wrong way. You mustn't get down about it. A person like that don't deserve to live. He's a lot better off dead than he is alive.

—Jim Thompson,
The Killer Inside Me, 1952

This was what I wanted, you see, the end. And it seemed like she should want it, too; that she should damned well get it, regardless of what she wanted. Because Fay wasn't fit to live, because she'd be better off dead or locked up for life. And I started to tell her that.

—Jim Thompson,
After Dark My Sweet, 1955

DELL
FIRST EDITION
B157
35¢
She couldn't run any more from the two men who wanted her— both for different reasons
CORNERED!
James McKimmey

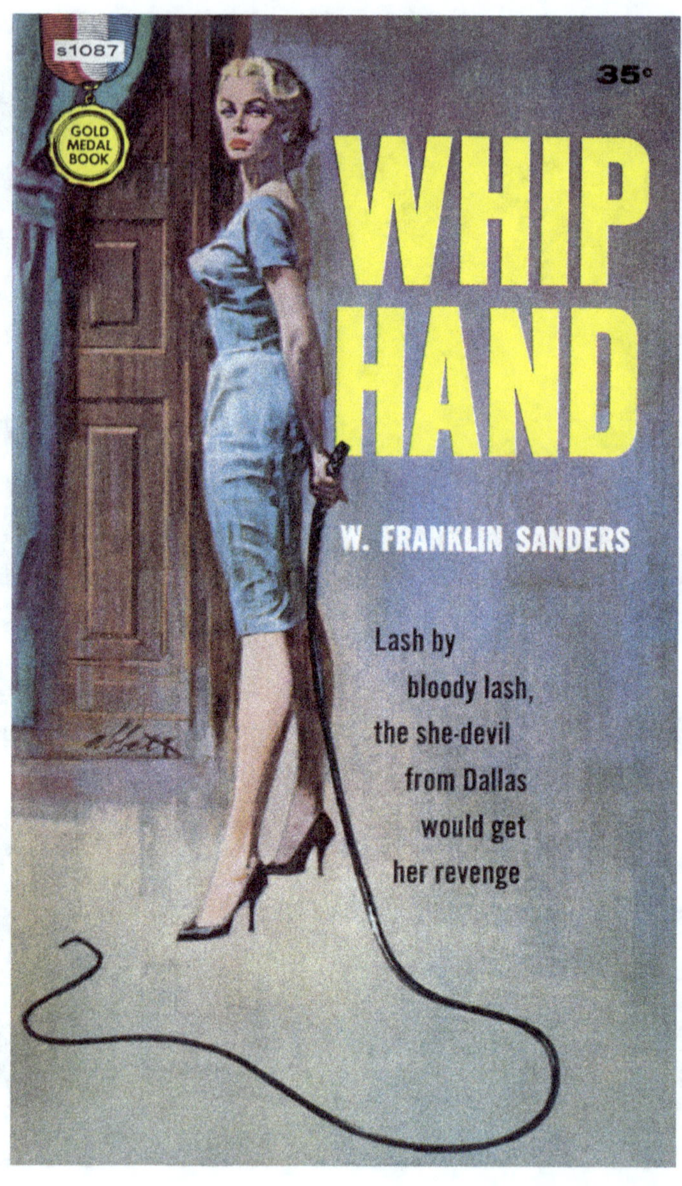
s1087
GOLD MEDAL BOOK
35¢
WHIP HAND
W. FRANKLIN SANDERS
Lash by bloody lash, the she-devil from Dallas would get her revenge

Her Eyes Had Pain in Them

There on the table was the gun, with the safety catch off and the silencer still attached. Those loving arms would have reached it nicely. A face that was waiting to be kissed was really waiting to be splattered with blood when she blew my head off. My blood. When I heard her fall I turned around. Her eyes had pain in them now, the pain preceding death. Pain and unbelief.

"How c-could you?" she gasped.

I only had a moment before talking to a corpse, but I got it in.

"It was easy," I said.

—Mickey Spillane,
I, the Jury, 1947

The hand had let his romance turn from guitar strumming to mauling me around quite a bit before I got away from him and ran into the house crying and yelping, with my denim shirt in tatters. The rest of the boys caught him before he got to the border and brought him back a few days later. Dad had been judge and jury, and the punishment still makes me shudder. But it had been thrilling and exciting, too. When the rash cowboy was able to travel again the boys escorted him to the border he had tried to make the first time. I felt sorry for him.

But I knew I would thrill at the sight of these kidnappers getting a taste of the whip! I went to the closet off the back hall and found the whip and took it to Dad. He fondled the short heavy handle, and I could guess his thoughts. With just a suggestion of motion he flicked the long lash across the room into the corner, like a striking snake. It was uncanny, his easy command of that writhing, searching coil. Deep inside me I felt a surge of fear mixed with pleasure.

—W. Frankin Sanders (with Charles Willeford),
Whip Hand, 1961

The bed rocked as if I were still driving, and the instant I closed my eyes the pulpy and battered mass of her face was burned into the backs of the lids down to the last projecting shard of bone, and I sat up shaking and sick, my mouth locked against the outcry welling up inside me.

—Charles Williams,
The Long Saturday Night, 1962

As Roy Dillon stumbled out of the shop his face was a sickish green, and each breath he drew was an incredible agony. A hard blow in the guts can do that to a man, and Dillon had gotten a hard one. Not with a fist, which would have been bad enough, but from the butt-end of a heavy club.

—Jim Thompson,
The Grifters, 1963

1990 ✱ ✱ 25¢
FREDRIC BROWN
ONE FOR THE ROAD
Murder, adultery and hidden lust— the story of a beautiful girl who knew too much about the wrong men
MOTEL
NO VACANCIES
A BANTAM MYSTERY

1007
GOLD MEDAL BOOK
The mob's law was inflexible.
You obeyed.
If not, they sent—
25c
THE ENFORCER
OVID DEMARIS

Out of the Sewer

I felt like a heel. All she had to do was look at me when I got that way and I felt like I was crawling up out of a sewer somewhere.

—Mickey Spillane,
Vengeance is Mine! 1950

They had to let him go since they couldn't book him on the general charge that he was another Hell's Kitchen rat come up out of the sewer.

—Benjamin Appel,
Life and Death of a Tough Guy, 1955

Billy grinned. "You know, baby, you're the prettiest target I ever had in my life?"

Gloria met his look unwaveringly. "Where do you find pretty things in sewers?"

—James McKimmey,
Cornered! 1960

It was such cool thinking that you would never imagine this guy to have clawed his way out of the sewer slums to make it this far.

—Mickey Spillane,
The Deep, 1961

You're a bastard, Parker. You're a rotten bastard. You're a filthy rotten son of a bitch. You take advantage of a poor old blind man, you'd spit on your own mother. You're a cesspool, a walking cesspool, you're vomit, you're a cheap two-bit rotten punk

—Richard Stark,
The Score, 1964

PYRAMID BOOKS R-730 50¢
Carley Mills
A NEAR-NESS OF EVIL
TWISTED PASSIONS, STRANGE DESIRES – THE SHATTERING NOVEL OF A BEAUTIFUL YOUNG BLUE-BLOOD AND HER SENSU-ALIST FATHER.
"Plunges you into a devil's world"
SAN FRANCISCO EXAMINER

950
GOLD MEDAL BOOK
25c
Backwoods Teaser
She wasn't exactly a tramp...
Gil Brewer
author of
13 FRENCH STREET

Black Coffee Hot as Hell

Estelle brought the coffee, thick as mud and hot as hell.

—Fredric Brown,
The Dead Ringer, 1948

I tried the coffee. It was strong as acid and hot as hell.

—Mickey Spillane,
The Big Kill, 1951

If you cannot stand the spoon upright in the cup, then the coffee is too weak. We have a saying, you know, that coffee must be "hot as hell, black as sin, and sweet as love."

—Lawrence Block,
The Thief Who Couldn't Sleep, 1966

"What time is it?" Carmalita yawned.

"Almost nine. I didn't mean to wake you."

"You didn't, silly. I'll fix you some breakfast."

"No," Donahue said. "Really, Carm. You lie there."

"At least some coffee. You always say you like my coffee." He loathed it. She prepared coffee Cuban style.

Carmalita sat up. The sheet fell to her waist.

Donahue felt a knife go through him. Her breasts loomed large as melons, and as firm. There were dimples in the olive of her shoulders. Her waist was incredibly tiny, swelling to magnificent hips. She had an unusual face, too irregular to be called beautiful, sultry, a unique enchantment, with a focal point of large soft lips, as richly red as her nipples were richly brown.

—Ellery Queen,
Who Spies, Who Kills, 1966

I drank the coffee black, and it was thick enough to slice with my knife.

—Charles Willeford,
Cockfighter, 1962

DELL
FIRST
EDITION
A114
A small-time tough
in a big-time world
25¢
THE BIG BITE
by the author of Gulf Coast Girl
CHARLES WILLIAMS

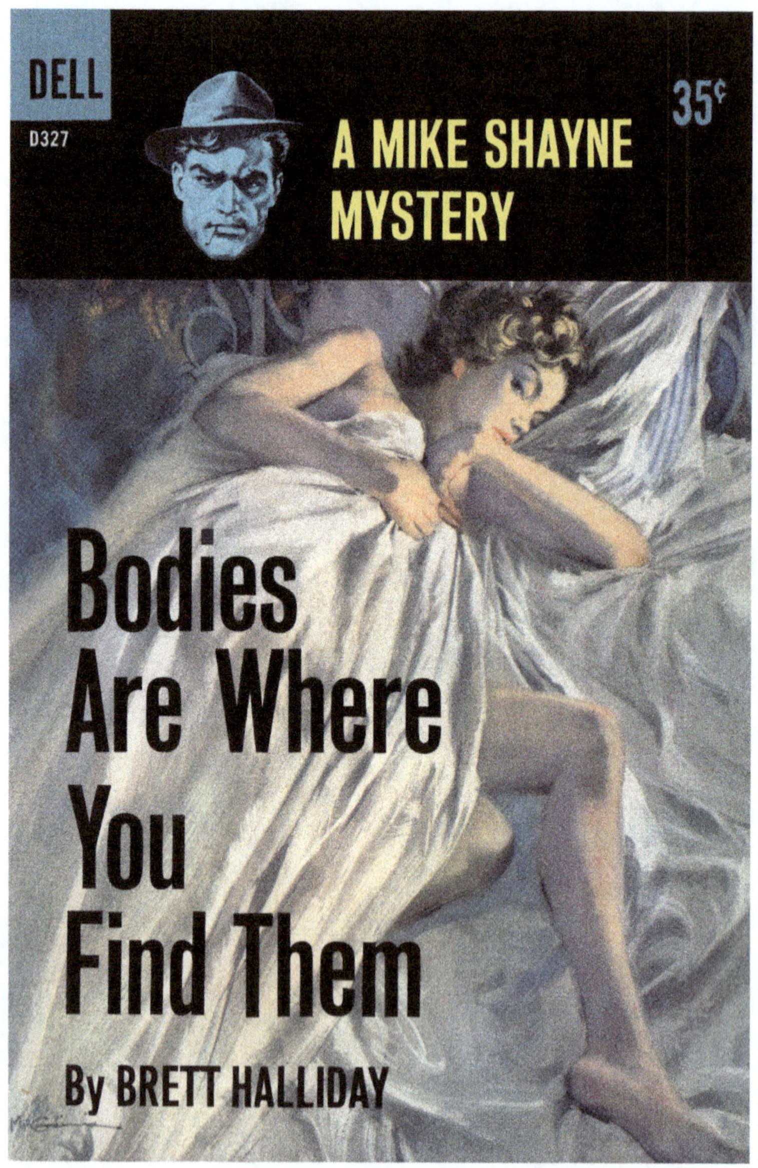
DELL
D327
35¢
A MIKE SHAYNE
MYSTERY
Bodies
Are Where
You
Find Them
By BRETT HALLIDAY

She's Old Enough to Be Your Wife

"Do you know Fay Estabrook?"

"A little. I passed her on the way up a few years ago. A few more years, and I'll pass her on the way down."

"Introduce me to her."

"Why?"

"I've always wanted to meet her."

"I don't get it, Lew. She's old enough to be your wife."

—Ross Macdonald,
The Moving Target, 1949

She had the kind of style that didn't go on with her make-up, and she was about my age. As a man gets older, if he knows what is good for him, the women he likes are getting older, too. The trouble is that most of them are married.

—Ross Macdonald,
The Zebra-Striped Hearse, 1962

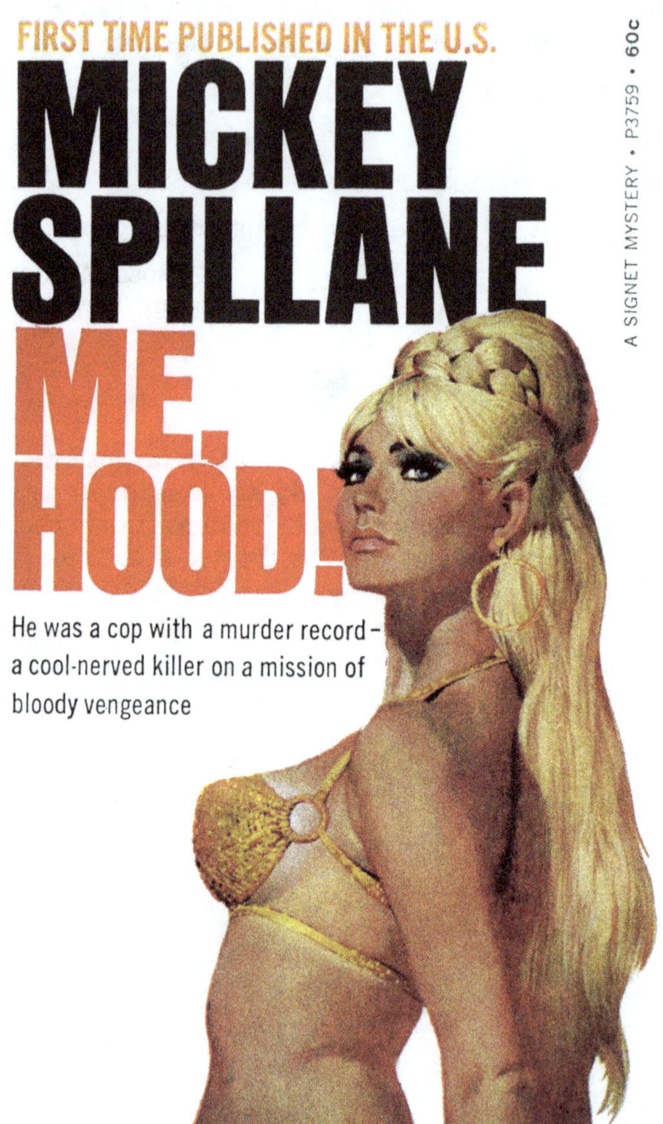
FIRST TIME PUBLISHED IN THE U.S.
MICKEY SPILLANE
ME, HOOD!
He was a cop with a murder record - a cool-nerved killer on a mission of bloody vengeance
A SIGNET MYSTERY • P3759 • 60c

GOLD MEDAL k1320
40c
color him dead
He escaped to a tropical island and met the native girl who could make a man forget anything—anything but the years he lost in prison for a murder he didn't commit
BY CHARLES RUNYON
author of THE DEATH CYCLE

35¢
s1161
GOLD MEDAL BOOK
Stag Preston, idol of millions—
whose private life was wilder than
any of the songs he sang
ROCKABILLY
HARLAN
ELLISON

A Sound of Distant Drums

"You know anybody named Cy Grildquist?"

"Sure," he said. "He's got a play on Broadway right now. A Sound of Distant Drums. A good money-maker."

—Donald Westlake,
The Mercenaries, 1960

There was a single bed in the back room, where the roommate slept when she was in town, and a studio couch in the living room, which was Anita's bed. The roommate now being out with the touring company of A Sound of Distant Drums, Anita had taken over the bedroom in the interim.

—Edwin West (Donald Westlake),
Young and Innocent, 1961

There was a book in my room that I hadn't finished yet, a novel by Ben Christopher called A Sound of Distant Drums. It wasn't the greatest thing since vaudeville but I managed to get lost in it and kill the too many hours before it was time to go to work.

—Andrew Shaw (Lawrence Block),
$20 Lust, 1961

He shot the rest of the afternoon at a movie. There was a double feature playing at a movie house on Broadway between 88th and 89th and he hadn't seen either picture, so he went.

One was a cops-and-robbers thing called The Mercenaries, and the screen credits said it was based on a book that had won the Edgar, whatever the hell that meant. The other was A Sound of Distant Drums and it was about a group of young actors and actresses trying to get ahead in Hollywood. It bored him stiff. He sat through both pictures waiting for them to end, munching popcorn and smoking cigarettes in direct violation of fire department rules and regulations.

—Andrew Shaw (Lawrence Block),
Lover, 1961

"We could go to the movies," he suggested. His tone seemed to indicate that he was not too keen on the idea.

"What's playing?"

"A western, I guess—Sound of Distant Drums. Something like that."

"Sounds lousy."

—Sheldon Lord (Lawrence Block),
April North, 1961

It was evening. Joe was lying on a bed, book in his hand, a western entitled A Sound of Distant Drums, by James Blue. Anita was sitting on the edge of the other bed and staring emptily across the room.

—Sheldon Lord (Lawrence Block),
Pads are for Passion, 1961

I dropped a buck for the drink and some change for the waiter on the table, and I left. Two blocks further along the Boardwalk I found a good restaurant where they served me a blood-rare steak and very black coffee. I lingered awhile over a second cup of coffee, then went out and found a movie.

The movie was lousy, a historical epic called A Sound of Distant Drums, a technicolor cinemascope package with pretty girls and flashing swords and people getting themselves killed flamboyantly. I dozed through most of it.

—Lawrence Block,
Mona, 1961

"What's at the movie?" she asked again, shrugging into her coat.

He shook his head. "Some dog called A Sound Of Distant Drums. It's either a Korean War thing or a Western, I forget."

—Edwin West (Donald Westlake),
Campus Doll, 1961

Grinnell was going to cast me for the Agatha part in 'A Sound of Distant Drums' but the angel decided that oil stocks looked better than off-Broadway ventures. Then I ran second in the last three auditions. But they don't pay off for second place."

—Lawrence Block,
Death Pulls a Doublecross, 1961

I leaned forward and read the title upside down. A Sound of Distant Drums. If It was a hit, it would be George's first.

—Donald Westlake,
Killing Time, 1961

The hack took Eighth Avenue. Johnny gazed out to the right, watching the throngs of people pouring out of the theaters along the side streets leading from Broadway. His eyes took in theater marquees: Up for Grabs—A Sound of Distant Drums—The Lonely. All good shows, and all drawing good audiences.

—Ben Christopher (Lawrence Block),
Strange Embrace,1962

Bill wanted to go to another movie that night, but I couldn't take it. So we sat around the room and drank and after a while I threw a gin hand out the window. A little after midnight, we went down to 42nd Street and saw an important movie that had been made from a Broadway play called A Sound of Distant Drums. It was about homosexuality and what a burden it was, but the hero bore the burden girlfully. It didn't convert me.

—Donald Westlake,
361, 1962

The decision to stay for dinner had been a pleasant one, suggested by Maggie and agreed to readily enough by Elly. They had had lunch, had shopped for awhile on Fifth Avenue without buying anything, then headed west to Broadway. A Sound Of Distant Drums, the hit drama based on the Westlake kidnaping, was playing at the Cort; for the hell of it, Maggie went to the box office to see if any tickets were available for that evening. There was a pair on hand, front and center in the orchestra.

—Sheldon Lord (Lawrence Block),
Community of Women, 1963

"I know you from someplace," and he remembered thinking, Jesus, maybe this guy is on the hot list. But Jerry had gripped and said, "I'm the guy shot June Havoc in The Sound of Distant Drums," and wasn't that L.A. for you? Your real estate man turns out to be a one-time actor.

—Donald Westlake,
The Comedy is Finished,
circa early-1980s, published 2012

Kelp turned right, drove downtown to Greenwich Village, turned left on 8th Street, and parked just shy of the theater, whose marquee advertised "American Premiere—A Sound of Distant Drums." That was the movie May had told Dortmunder she intended to see tonight, telling him about it last night, making small talk while Dortmunder's hand had soaked in the Palmolive Liquid.

—Donald Westlake,
Why Me? 1983

GOLD MEDAL k1522
40c
THE KILLER INSIDE ME
BY JIM THOMPSON
"Probably the most chilling and believable first-person story of a criminally warped mind I have ever encountered."—Stanley Kubrick
"Jim Thompson is the best suspense writer going, bar none."
—George Milburn, THE NEW YORK TIMES

PETER RABE
996
GOLD MEDAL BOOK
25c
MURDER ME FOR NICKELS
I'm the guy who sees that the right jukeboxes get played. Ours. Otherwise, 5¢ can get you murder with your music

CHESTER HIMES
author of The Big Gold Dream
AVON
35c
T-434
ALL SHOT UP
BAR
Coffin Ed and Grave Digger beat a path through babes, bourbon and bullets on the trail of an ice-cold killer
"... the most original new detective pair in modern fiction"
Clark Kinnaird, Parade of Books
An Avon Original

Acknowledgements

Special thanks to the members of the RARA-AVIS internet board especially David Rachels, Bill Crider, Charles Ardai, Michael S. Chong. Timothy J. Lockhart, Ron Clinton, Mark Nevins and the late Mario Taboada (1957-2010) and Michael R. Robinson (1954-2007).

DELL
FIRST EDITION
B220
Robert Flick discovers that when a dame's too hot to handle, she'll blaze away at you—with a loaded gun.
35¢
SLOW BURN
By Jack Ehrlich
"...parole officer Robert Flick is a flic with character who would be worth meeting again."
—Anthony Boucher, THE NEW YORK TIMES

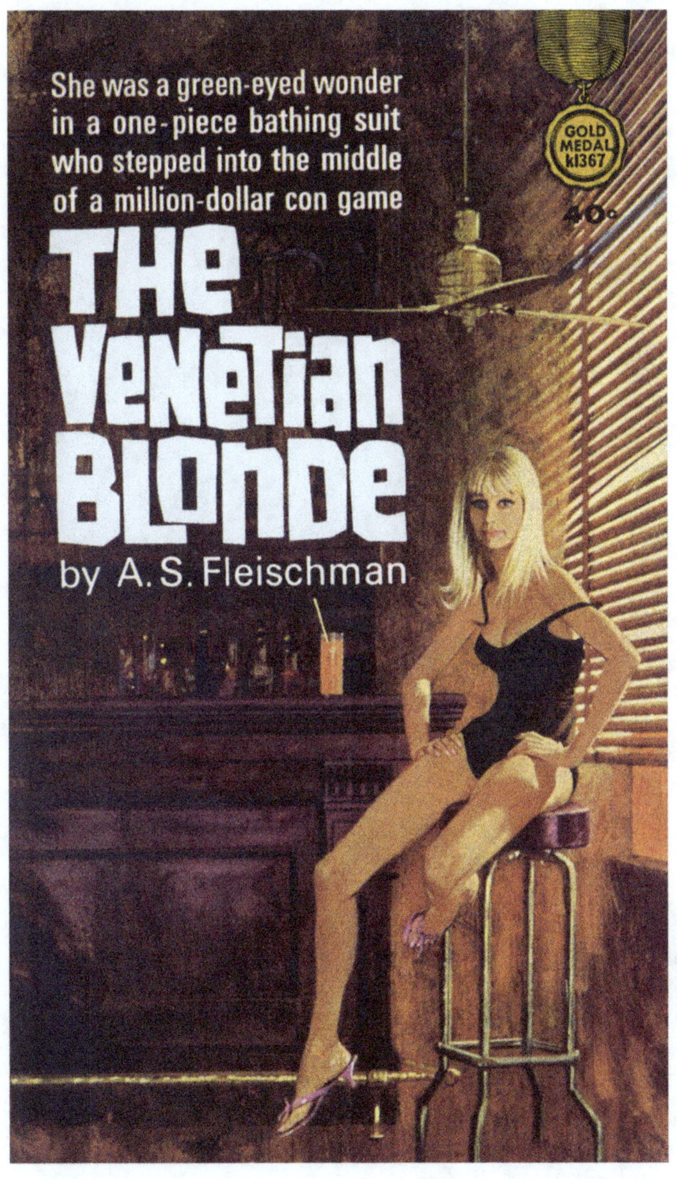
She was a green-eyed wonder
in a one-piece bathing suit
who stepped into the middle
of a million-dollar con game
THE
VENETIAN
BLONDE
by A. S. Fleischman
GOLD
MEDAL
k1367
40¢

GOLD MEDAL k1310
40¢
By BASIL HEATTER
Virgin Cay
Author of
THE TROUBLE WITH LOVE
and THE DIM VIEW
Marooned on a barren sandspit by a hired
killer who was too soft to do
the job quickly...

About the Editor

Jeff Vorzimmer started his career in Wall Street writing press releases. He then transitioned to publishing and has spent nearly 20 years with The Austin American-Statesman in Austin, Texas. He is currently at work on a book about his father entitled, Tales of the Living Legend.

He drinks his rye whisky straight and his coffee black.

www.ingramcontent.com/pod-product-compliance
Lightning Source LLC
Chambersburg PA
CBHW071006120726
47910CB00004B/1401

* 9 7 8 0 9 9 7 0 1 5 0 3 4 *